MW00899931

See with Your Ears!

Dolphin and Bat Echolocation

This course was written by
Naturally Curious Expert

Kira Freed

*Kira used to be an archaeozoologist. Now she
writes science materials for children. She is curious
about all the different forms of life in our world.*

Copyright © 2014 by Be Naturally Curious, LLC.

All rights reserved. No part of this publication may be reproduced, distributed,
or transmitted in any form or by any means, including photocopying, recording, or other
electronic or mechanical methods, without the prior written permission of the publisher.

Printed by CreateSpace

ISBN 978-1-942403-01-2

www.benaturallycurious.com

Many activities in this book make use of printed materials. If you prefer not to cut them directly from this book, please visit the URL listed below and enter the code for a supplemental PDF containing all printable materials.

URL: www.benaturallycurious.com/echolocation-printables/

password: **bats**

Table of Contents

Required Materials

- Blindfold, such as a scarf or headband
- Paper towel tube (optional)
- Aluminum pie plate (optional)
- Blank sheets of paper
- Blanket

- Hat or scarf that covers the ears
- Pen or pencil
- Crayons, colored pencils, or markers
- Masking tape
- Stapler (optional)
- Scissors

© Be Naturally Curious, LLC. All rights reserved.

Dolphin and Bat School: Learn to Echolocate!

BEVERLY BAT: Welcome, students! I'm Beverly Bat, and this is my friend Darius Dolphin. We're here today to give you your first lesson in a topic that will be very important to you for your whole lives—ECHOLOCATION! Who knows what echolocation is?

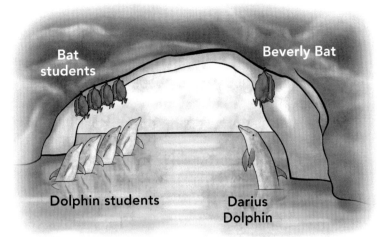

BAT STUDENT: Is it something about locating echoes?

BEVERLY BAT: Great guess! Echolocation has two parts. The first part is about sending out sound waves so they'll bounce off things and come back to you. The second part is about hearing the sounds that echo back and understanding what they mean. Check out these diagrams of how echolocation works.

Can you trace the route of the sound waves with your finger in each diagram below? Which color shows sound waves going away from the dolphin? Which color shows sound waves coming back from the fish?

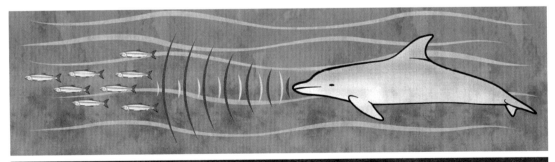

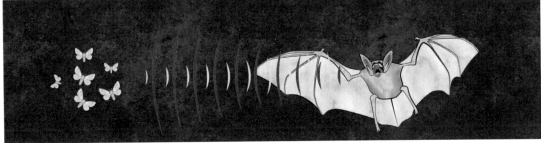

© Be Naturally Curious, LLC. All rights reserved.

BAT STUDENT: Wait a minute! What exactly are sound waves, and how do they move?

DARIUS DOLPHIN: Great questions! Sound is a type of energy that is made by vibrations. When things VIBRATE, they move back and forth quickly. For example, if a piece of rock drops from the roof of the cave into the water, tiny particles in the water where it fell start to vibrate. Those vibrations make the tiny particles next to them vibrate, and then the particles next to *them* vibrate. Sound moves out from where it was first made in SOUND WAVES. Sound moves through air, water, and even solid objects! Now that you know about sound waves, does anyone know why you'd want to send out sound waves and hear echoes?

> When things *vibrate*, they move back and forth quickly.

> Sound waves are waves of vibrating tiny particles that move through air, liquids, or solid objects.

DOLPHIN STUDENT: I don't need to know about all this until I grow up, but I want to know NOW!

DARIUS: And I'd be glad to tell you! All of you are in this class because you're ready to move on to a new stage in your lives. Up to this point, your parents have been helping you with everything—finding food for you, showing you where to go, and taking care of all your needs. The time has come to learn how to take care of yourselves.

BAT STUDENT (crying): Do we HAVE to? I don't want to!!

DARIUS: It makes complete sense that you might feel unsure of yourselves. This is a very big change for all of you! But Beverly and I are going to do our best to teach you step by step, and you'll get lots of practice in class. Before you know it, you'll be experts. Beverly, let's start with some fun so we can get our students excited about what they're learning.

BEVERLY: I love practicing my fancy aerobatic moves. Now, who wants to join me?

BAT STUDENTS: I do! I do! I do!

BEVERLY: Okay, let's fly!!

© Be Naturally Curious, LLC. All rights reserved.

DOLPHIN STUDENTS: We want to fly, too!

DARIUS: We dolphins don't fly in the air, but we sure can fly through the water—and leap, too. Let's go!

BEVERLY: Okay! Now let's settle down so Darius and I can teach you about echolocation. Let's think about Darius's question from earlier: Does anyone know *why* you'd want to send out sounds and make meaning from their echoes? No guesses? Well, there are two big reasons, and they're the same reasons whether you're a bat or a dolphin. The first reason is to find food, and the second reason is to NAVIGATE—to know where you're going when you fly or swim around.

DARIUS: That's right, Beverly. And the reason you need to use echolocation to find food and know where you're going is—

DOLPHIN STUDENT (with raised flipper): "Because it's dark!"

DARIUS: Very good!! For bats, it's dark because you're active at night, and for dolphins, it's dark because we often swim underwater where sunlight doesn't reach. As a result, we can't rely on our eyesight. Echolocation is an extra sense that some animals have—some bats, dolphins and their cousins, and a few other animals. Here's how it works. Let's say Beverly is hungry—

> When animals *navigate*, they figure out where they're going as they move around their surroundings.

© Be Naturally Curious, LLC. All rights reserved.

BEVERLY: I'm *always* hungry! Please excuse me for a moment while I go find a tasty bug.

DARIUS: Yes, of course . . . So Beverly makes some clicks with her LARYNX that go out through her mouth. (In humans, the larynx is a hollow organ in the throat that holds the VOCAL CORDS, which are used for talking.) Some bats also have a fleshy structure on their nose called a NOSELEAF. A noseleaf helps a bat send clicks in the direction it wants them to go. Anyway, once Beverly makes some clicks, they go out in the direction she sends them, and they bounce off nearby objects. If the sounds bounce off a moth, what do you think happens?

BEVERLY: Dinner! Awesome!!

DARIUS: Please, Beverly—I was asking our students.

BEVERLY: Oh, sorry. I couldn't help myself. I *love* moths!

A *larynx*, or voice box, is an organ in the throat of some animals that is involved in making sounds and breathing.

The *vocal cords* are folds of tissue in the larynx that are used to produce sound when air causes them to vibrate.

A bat's *noseleaf* helps it send sound in a chosen direction.

BAT NOSELEAVES

Greater
spear-nosed bat

Northern little
yellow-eared bat

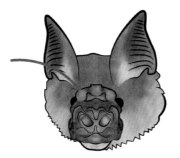

Asian
leaf-nosed bat

© Be Naturally Curious, LLC. All rights reserved.

DARIUS: Okay, students—so Beverly sends out some clicks, and they bounce off a moth that's close to her. Now she has to hear those echoes. Lucky for her, she's got magnificent ears. Check out Beverly's ears, everyone!

DARIUS: Do you see those long, pointed skin flaps in the middle of Beverly's ears? Each one of those is called a TRAGUS (TRAY-gus). When echoes reach the tragus, they then travel to special cells in her inner ear. As a result, Beverly can tell how far away the moth is. She can also tell how big it is, which way it's going, and how fast it's moving. Then she knows exactly how to catch it. Pretty amazing, isn't it?

A *tragus* is a fleshy skin flap on a bat's outer ear that helps it hear echoing sounds.

BEVERLY: Now it's time for all bat students to practice your clicks.

BAT STUDENT: I already know how to do that. I like to click when my dad is taking a nap. It's funny to see him get confused. He thinks he's having an echolocation dream, but then he realizes he's not.

BEVERLY: Well, since you're so smart, why don't you come to the front of the cave and lead your friends in practicing their clicks. Pay attention, young bats, to the echoes you hear.

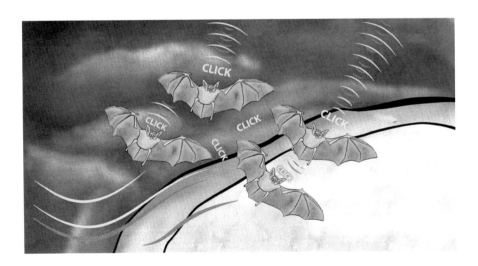

BAT ECHOLOCATION

Making Sounds	Hearing Sounds
Clicks are made in the larynx and usually sent out through the mouth.	Clicks are heard with the help of each ear's tragus, which sends sounds to the inner ear.

© Be Naturally Curious, LLC. All rights reserved.

Trace the **pink line** with your finger to follow the sound being made.
Trace the blue line with your finger to follow the sound being heard.

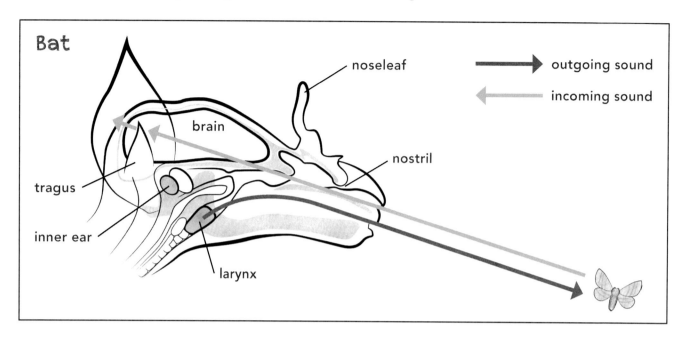

BEVERLY: Okay, now let's talk about dolphin clicks. Dolphins make clicking noises by passing air up toward their **BLOWHOLE**. That's the hole in the top of their head that's used for breathing. As the air travels, it's forced through a structure called the **PHONIC LIPS**. That's a funny name for a very important body part—and it's *not* for kissing!

DARIUS: My phonic lips are in a part of my head that's sort of like a human's nasal passages, where air travels after it's breathed in through a person's nose. When I send air through my passageway, my phonic lips are sucked together, and the tissue around them vibrates. The vibrations travel into my head to another special part called the **MELON**, which is in my forehead. The melon makes the vibrations into a beam of sound that I send out.

BAT STUDENT: So how do you hear the echoes from your clicks? You don't appear to have any ears.

BEVERLY: You're so right. Not every animal is fortunate enough to have my glorious ears, but Darius, the poor dear, is still an expert at hearing dolphin clicks. He has special material around and in his lower jaw that sends sounds to his middle ears.

A whale's or dolphin's *blowhole* is a breathing hole, similar to a human's nostril, located at the top of its head.

When air passes through a whale's or dolphin's *phonic lips*, they vibrate.

A whale's or dolphin's *melon*, located in its forehead, focuses vibrations from the phonic lips into a beam of sound.

© Be Naturally Curious, LLC. All rights reserved.

DARIUS: That's right. So let's say I'm hungry—

BEVERLY: Don't say *hungry*, Darius! Now I have to excuse myself and go get a snack. Click, click, click!

DARIUS: Beverly, please control yourself—the students are getting distracted! Pay attention, class. So let's say I'm hungry, and I want to find some fish. As I'm swimming around, I send out some clicks, and they bounce off a fish. My echolocation is just as accurate and helpful as Beverly's. I can tell how far away the fish is, how big it is, which way it's going, and how fast it's moving. That information helps me know whether it's a medium-sized fish I want to eat for lunch or a huge fish—such as a shark—that I need to get away from fast.

DOLPHIN ECHOLOCATION

Making Sounds	Hearing Sounds
Clicks are made by the phonic lips and sent to the melon, where they are focused into a beam of sound.	Clicks are heard with the help of fatty tissue around and in the lower jaw, which sends sounds to the middle ears.

Trace the pink line with your finger to follow the sound being made.
Trace the blue line with your finger to follow the sound being heard.

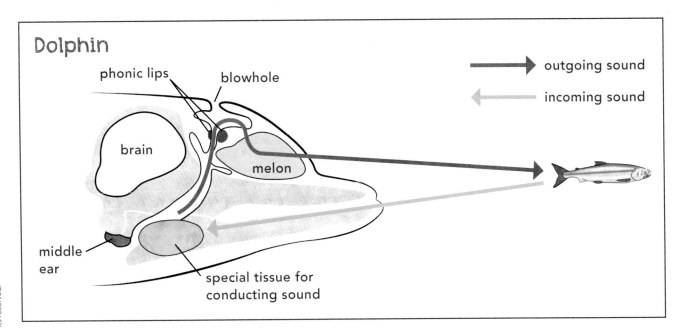

© Be Naturally Curious, LLC. All rights reserved.

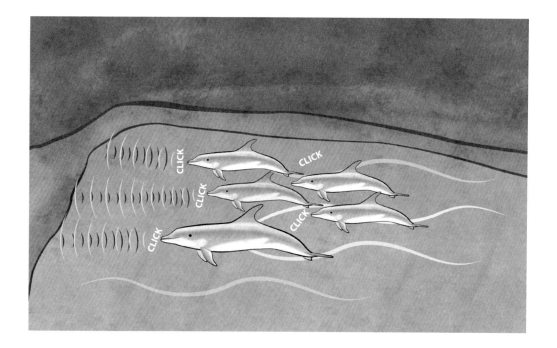

DARIUS: Okay, dolphin students. Now it's time to practice our clicks. Aim them at the rock wall of the cave, and see what happens.

DARIUS: What did you notice, class?

DOLPHIN STUDENT: I heard echoes! It works!

DARIUS: That's right, and I'm glad to see your excitement. I *told* you it was fun! And just wait until you start using it to get food and find your way around!

BEVERLY: Okay, class—it's time for our lunch break. Darius and I have a little assignment for you. Practice sending out clicks and listening for echoes. See what you discover— and what you catch for lunch! Louder echoes come from bigger objects, while softer echoes come from smaller objects. If you hear the echoes on one side more than the other, you'll know which side the object is on. Be sure to stay close to the cave. When we gather again after lunch, I'm sure you'll all have some exciting stories about your new abilities!

© Be Naturally Curious, LLC. All rights reserved.

How Do You Hear?

ACTIVITY 1

In the story, you read about how bats and dolphins hear echolocation clicks. Check out the charts below, as well as the chart of how humans hear. How is human hearing similar to bat hearing and dolphin hearing? How is it different?

In each diagram, trace the route of the sound waves and name the different body parts each animal uses to hear. You will even find out what YOU use to hear!

Bat

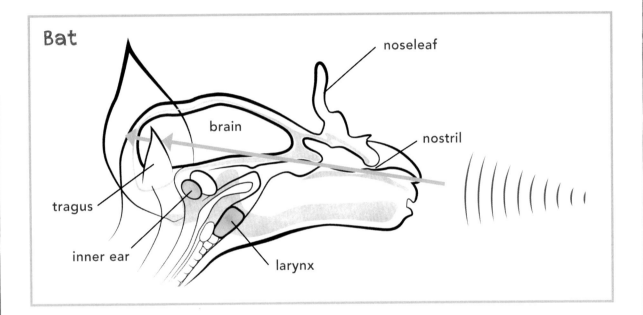

Dolphin

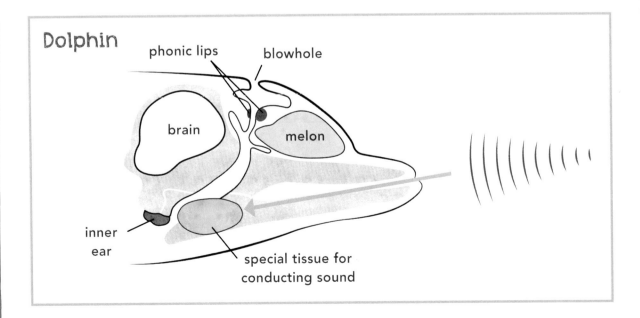

© Be Naturally Curious, LLC. All rights reserved.

ACTIVITY
1

How Do You Hear?

(continued)

Human

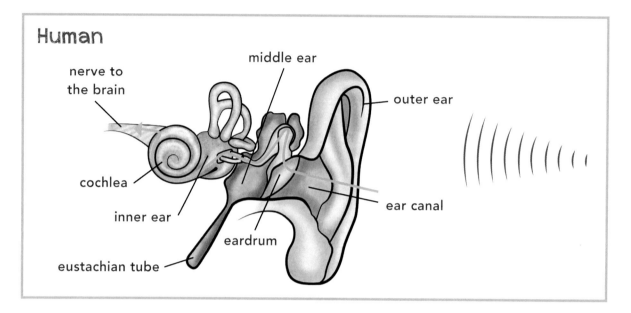

You live with your ears every day, and you may not give a lot of thought to your hearing. Would you like to pretend that you have bat or dolphin hearing instead? We'll also include orcas in this activity since they echolocate, too!

INSTRUCTIONS

1. Decide whether you want to be a bat, dolphin, or orca.

   • As a bat, you'll be making a new set of ears since bats rely on their ears for hearing. You can choose the ears of a spotted bat or a California leaf-nosed bat.

   • As a dolphin or orca, you'll be making a snout since these animals use their jaws to help them hear.

2. Color and then cut out the cutouts for the animal you chose. Keep in mind that each bat ear has two parts—the main ear and the tragus. The dolphin and orca snouts each have two parts. You can use the examples as a guide for coloring or make up your own pattern of color!

3. For the headband, cut out several long strips of blank

MATERIALS

• Cutouts for bat ears (pages 29–33)

• Cutout for dolphin snout (pages 35–37)

• Cutout for orca snout (pages 39–41)

• Blank sheets of paper

• Crayons, colored pencils, or markers

• Masking tape

• Stapler (optional)

• Scissors

© Be Naturally Curious, LLC. All rights reserved.

How Do You Hear?

(continued)

paper roughly two inches wide. Tape or staple them together at one end. TIP: The folded tips of the staples should be facing *away* from the hair or skin.

4. For bat ears:

a) Line up the dotted lines on each tragus/ear pair. Tape or staple each tragus to an ear with the tragus in front and the colored sides facing outward.

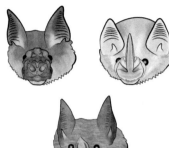

line up the
dotted lines

b) Then attach the ears to the headband.

c) Gently roll the loose end of each tragus around your finger to curl it and make it stand away from the main ear behind it.

d) Ask an adult to help you decide how tightly to attach the two ends of the headband so the bat ears will stay on your head. Then use tape or staples to connect the two ends.

For a dolphin or orca snout:

a) Place the wide end of the upper half of the snout over your nose as in this diagram. Place the wide end of the lower half under your chin. The sides of the two pieces should overlap below your ears or along the back end of your cheeks.

b) Ask an adult to help you decide how much the two pieces should overlap on each side for a good fit. Then tape or staple the overlapping pieces. If you use tape, place it on the uncolored side so it won't show.

c) With an adult's help, use tape or staples to firmly attach one side of the headband to the snout.

d) Use masking tape to attach the other side of the headband to the snout so your creation can be taken on and off.

© Be Naturally Curious, LLC. All rights reserved.

ACTIVITY
1

How Do You Hear?

(continued)

5. Check out how you look as bat, dolphin, or orca in a mirror. What do you think?

6. Now it's time to become the animal whose hearing you're trying out! If you're a bat, "fly" around making clicks and imagine using your fantastic ears to hear the echoes. If you're a dolphin or orca, click away as you "swim" and imagine the echoes coming back to your jaws and then traveling to your inner ears. Have fun navigating and catching food!

Who Echolocates?

Bats and dolphins are the best-known echolocators, but they're not the only ones! Four groups of animals echolocate.

- **Bats:** Scientists often divide bats into two groups: microbats and megabats. Most microbats eat insects and use echolocation to get their food. Microbats may also be called true bats. (Megabats, also called fruit bats, eat fruit and/or flower nectar.) Microbats are usually, but not always, smaller than megabats.

- **Dolphins and their cousins:** Dolphins are actually a type of toothed whale. Whales are divided into two groups: toothed whales (whales with teeth) and baleen (buh-LEEN or bay-LEEN) whales. Toothed whales are the echolocators. Different types of toothed whales use echolocation to find different types of food, including fish, squid, octopuses, seals, and more. (Instead of teeth, baleen whales have a material like fingernails, called baleen, along their upper jaw. These whales take in huge mouthfuls of water and then push it out through the baleen, which traps tiny animals against the sides of the whales' mouths.)

- **Shrews and tenrecs:** Besides bats and whales, two other groups of mammals echolocate. Shrews look similar to moles, and tenrecs look similar to hedgehogs. These small animals produce squeaks instead of clicks. They use echolocation to find their way but not to find food.

- **A few types of birds:** Two types of birds—oilbirds and some swiftlets—use a simple form of echolocation. They make calls while they're flying to help them navigate through caves and trees. Both types of birds are active at night.

- **Some people:** Some blind people have learned how to use echolocation to help them find their way. Amazing!

© Be Naturally Curious, LLC. All rights reserved.

Echolocation Elements Game

ACTIVITY
2

Would you like to play a game about echolocation? This game involves all the elements, or different things, that are needed for bat and dolphin echolocation to work. Echolocation only happens when the elements come together!

Echolocation ELEMENTS

Element	Bats	Dolphins
Body part for creating sounds	• Larynx, or voice box* • Noseleaf* *Collect both parts to win!	• Phonic lips* • Melon* *Collect both parts to win!
Sound	• Bat clicks	• Dolphin clicks
Body parts for hearing echoes	• Tragus* • Special cells in the inner ear* *Collect both parts to win!	• Fatty structures around the lower jaw* • Special cells in the middle ear* * Collect both parts to win!
Purposes for echolocating** **Collect any two of the four purposes to win!	• Safe in a cave • Moth • Mosquito • Beetle	• Safe in the pod, or group • Fish • Squid • Shrimp

© Be Naturally Curious, LLC. All rights reserved.

ACTIVITY
2

Echolocation Elements Game

INSTRUCTIONS

Object of the game:

To collect all the necessary elements for successful echolocation in EITHER bats or dolphins

The play:

During the course of the game, players collect cards that correspond to the echolocation elements in the chart above. To win, players must fill up all the dolphin or bat spaces to collect a complete sequence of echolocation elements for one of these animals:

- two body parts for making sounds
- a sound
- two body parts for hearing echoes
- two purposes for echolocating

Here's an example of a winning card sequence:

MATERIALS

- One scorecard for each player (pages 43–45)
- Set of game cards (pages 47–51)
- Scissors

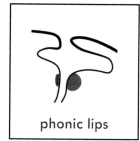
phonic lips

Body part 1 for
creating sounds

melon

Body part 2 for
creating sounds

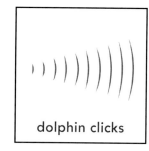
dolphin clicks

Sound

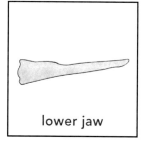
lower jaw

Body part 1 for
hearing echoes

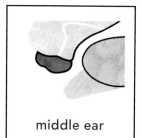
middle ear

Body part 2 for
hearing echoes

Safe in the pod
(group)

Purpose 1
for echolocating

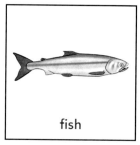
fish

Purpose 2
for echolocating

© Be Naturally Curious, LLC. All rights reserved.

ACTIVITY
2

Echolocation Elements Game

(continued)

1. Cut out the playing cards on pages 47–51 and mix them up. Place them face down on the table or other playing surface. If you can see the images through the back, place the cards in a bag that can be passed from player to player.

2. Each player gets a scorecard. One section of the scorecard is for bat "elements," and the other section is for dolphin "elements." Each player's cards go in the appropriate section of his or her scorecard. Players collect echolocation elements for both animals without planning which animal they hope to collect all the cards for, similar to placing markers on all Bingo squares without knowing which column or row will fill first.

3. Player 1 draws the top card from the pile or a card from the bag, reads it aloud, and places it in the correct place on his or her scorecard. If all spots for that type of card are full, he or she returns the card to the bottom of the pile. Player 2 then takes a turn, and the play continues.

4. Do you remember reading about "echolocation jamming" on page 23 of the Name That Sound activity? This game has a **JAM!** card. If you draw it, you can place it on top of any one card on an opponent's scorecard. Then both cards are returned to the pile, and the pile is shuffled well.

5. The first player to collect all the echolocation elements for one animal or the other calls out BAT! or DOLPHIN! and wins the game. The winner explains to the other player(s) the winning combination of echolocation elements. If there are enough players, the other players may choose to keep playing until someone collects all the cards for the other animal.

For a longer game:

Collect the elements for both a bat and a dolphin!

© Be Naturally Curious, LLC. All rights reserved.

ACTIVITY 3

Name That Sound

Echolocation allows bats and dolphins to navigate and find food using their ears instead of their eyes. Now that you've learned how bats and dolphins echolocate, it's time to try it out for yourself! Listen for different kinds of sounds without relying on your eyes to help you. You may be surprised at how much you normally use your eyes to help you hear!

INSTRUCTIONS

1. Pair up with two friends or family members. The three people will take turns being in three different roles: listener, soundmaker, and scribe (writer). Decide who will be in each role first.

2. The scribe takes one copy of the Experimental Journal and writes the listener's name at the top. During the experiment, the scribe will list each sound made by the soundmaker and record whether the listener identified the sound correctly and other details that are listed in the Experimental Journal.

3. The listener puts on the blindfold. He or she can either be sitting or standing during the listening activity.

4. The soundmaker creates different sounds in different locations within hearing range of the listener. The soundmaker creates three sounds from the suggestions below and/or other sounds not on the list.

   - clicking with the tongue
   - clapping
   - whistling
   - crumpling up a piece of paper
   - sliding the palms of the hands back and forth together
   - making any of the above sounds under a blanket
   - directing any of the above sounds through a tube, such as a paper towel tube
   - directing any of the above sounds through a tube toward an aluminum pie plate

MATERIALS

- Blindfold, such as a scarf or headband
- Paper towel tube (optional)
- Aluminum pie plate (optional)
- Several pieces of paper
- Blanket
- Hat or scarf that covers the ears
- Three copies of Experimental Journal (pages 53–57)
- Pen or pencil

© Be Naturally Curious, LLC. All rights reserved.

Name That Sound

INSTRUCTIONS (continued)

TIP: If the experiments are conducted indoors, the soundmaker will need to tiptoe or take off his or her shoes so the listener doesn't hear him or her walk in a certain direction, or the scribe can make noise while the soundmaker is changing direction.

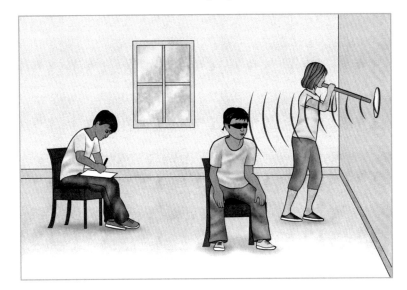

5. After each sound, the listener states his or her best guess about:

   • how the sound was made

   • which direction the sound came from (young kids can point)

   • how far away the sound was made (young kids can use units such as halfway across the room, all the way across the room, and so on)

   • anything else he or she notices about the sound

   The scribe records all this information in the Experimental Journal. NOTE: This process should be done silently. The focus is on setting up a careful experiment and recording the results. There will be time to share experiences later.

6. The listener removes the blindfold. Then the listener, soundmaker, and scribe rotate roles and repeat the experiment.

7. The listener removes the blindfold. Then the listener, soundmaker, and scribe rotate roles and repeat the experiment so everyone has a turn in each role.

8. Now sit together with your Experimental Journals in front of you and share your experiences. As the listener, how accurate were you in your guesses about the sounds you heard? As the

© Be Naturally Curious, LLC. All rights reserved.

ACTIVITY
3

Name That Sound

(continued)

soundmaker, how easy or hard was it to make sounds? As the scribe, how well were you able to record information in a careful, detailed way?

9. In the days and weeks to come, listen extra carefully to notice the sounds around you. How were those sounds created? What can you learn from them?

For parents:

• Children will learn a lot about sound and hearing by conducting these experiments at a range of distances. The soundmaker can initially choose one sound to make at, for example, 4 feet, 8 feet, 12 feet, 16 feet, and 20 feet from the listener. That will establish a general range that works with the listener's hearing levels.

• Humans are used to measuring sounds in terms of loudness, but there are many other qualities that also influence how well a sound is heard. For example, our ears are more sensitive to high sounds, which may seem louder than low sounds of the same intensity. Children can experiment with different qualities of sound, such as clapping (sharp) versus sliding the palms back and forth together (dull) and high sounds (for example, whistling) versus low sounds (for example, tapping a foot on the floor). In preparation for this activity, you might suggest that children go off by themselves and experiment with ways to make sounds that are loud, soft, high, low, sharp, dull, and other opposites they can think of.

• Note that individual listeners may vary in the distances and types of sounds they're able to hear clearly. Make sure children are respectful when communicating with each other about any hearing limitations.

For an extra challenge:

• Have the listener wear a hat or scarf that completely covers his or her ears.

• Think about ways to create sounds that will stump your friends with regard to where they're coming from or how they were created.

• Do the experiment in a location with background noise. Indoor options include music, a white noise machine, or a washing machine, dryer, or dishwasher. Possible outdoor options are traffic, construction noise, or a lawn mower. Read about "echolocation jamming" below to learn about similar echolocation challenges in nature.

© Be Naturally Curious, LLC. All rights reserved.

Name That Sound

(continued)

Echolocation Jamming

Echolocation jamming is anything that interferes with an animal's ability to echolocate. The jamming can come from any one of three sources:

- **The animal itself:** Jamming can happen if an animal is still making sounds when the echoes return. To keep this from happening, bats make shorter sounds as they get closer to their targets, and they wait until echoes come back before making another sound.

- **Other animals creating similar sounds nearby:** It's possible that several animals echolocating near each other could get confused by the similar sounds. To avoid this, bats change their clicks to make them a little different from the clicks of their close neighbors. Some bats instead get quiet and can sometimes catch an insect that another bat is tracking. Dolphins also go silent sometimes—not to steal each other's food but rather as a way of sharing information. If several dolphins are traveling together, they can save energy by listening to one dolphin's echoes, and no one gets confused from too many echoes. In dolphins, this process is called "echoic eavesdropping." (In humans, *eavesdropping* means secretly listening to a conversation.)

- **Prey (the animals being hunted by the echolocating animal):** Tiger moths make clicks in response to bat clicks. Most tiger moths are just warning bats that they taste bad. However, one type of tiger moth is trying to confuse bats, and it's quite successful! It's the only animal scientists know of that is able to jam its hunter's echolocation.

© Be Naturally Curious, LLC. All rights reserved.

Curiosity Connector

Here are some links to help you follow your curiosity!

- Check out cool echolocation video clips here:

  http://www.bbc.co.uk/learningzone/clips/dolphins-use-sonar-to-locate-food/10503.html

  and here:

  http://www.bbc.co.uk/learningzone/clips/bats-catch-fish-using-echolocation/10517.html

- Would you like to learn more about bats? Find answers to your questions here:

  http://www.kidzone.ws/ANIMALS/bats/index.htm

  and here:

  http://www.bats4kids.org/

- Learn neat facts about dolphins here:

  http://kids.nationalgeographic.com/animals/bottlenose-dolphin.html

  and here:

  http://www.sciencekids.co.nz/sciencefacts/animals/dolphin.html

- Are you curious about how blind people use echolocation? Check out this video clip:

  http://www.maniacworld.com/Blind-Kid-Uses-Echo-Location.html

  and this one:

  http://channel.nationalgeographic.com/channel/brain-games/videos/echolocation/

© Be Naturally Curious, LLC. All rights reserved.

Tools for Your Tool Kit

Let's make the ideas you learned today part of your life tool kit. Remember to print out some blank tool kit pages and tape or glue on today's tools.

1. Bats and dolphins live much of their lives in the dark. They send out sounds and listen for returning sounds for two main reasons:

   to _____ and _____ .

   Add ECHOLOCATION to your tool kit!

2. Name the two special body parts that bats use to send out sounds:

   _____ and _____

   Add LARYNX and NOSELEAF to your tool kit!

3. Name the two special body parts that dolphins use to send out sounds:

   _____ and _____

   Add PHONIC LIPS and MELON to your tool kit!

4. The opening at the top of a dolphin's head used for breathing is called a

   _____ .

   Add BLOWHOLE to your tool kit!

© Be Naturally Curious, LLC. All rights reserved.

Glossary

BLOWHOLE – a breathing hole at the top of a dolphin's or whale's head

ECHOLOCATION – a way to locate objects that involves sending out sounds and gathering information from the returning echoes

LARYNX – an organ in the throat of some animals that is involved in making sounds and breathing

MELON – a body part in a dolphin's or whale's head that focuses vibrations into a beam of sound

NAVIGATE – to find one's way over or through an area

NOSELEAF – a fleshy structure on the nose of some bats that helps them send sounds in a certain direction

PHONIC LIPS – a structure below the blowhole of echolocating dolphins and whales that vibrates when air passes through it

SOUND WAVES – waves of vibrating tiny particles that move through air, liquids, or solid objects

TRAGUS – a fleshy skin flap on a bat's outer ear that helps it hear echoing sounds

VIBRATE – to move back and forth quickly

VOCAL CORDS – folds of tissue in the larynx that are used to produce sound when air causes them to vibrate

© Be Naturally Curious, LLC. All rights reserved.

Greater spear-nosed bat

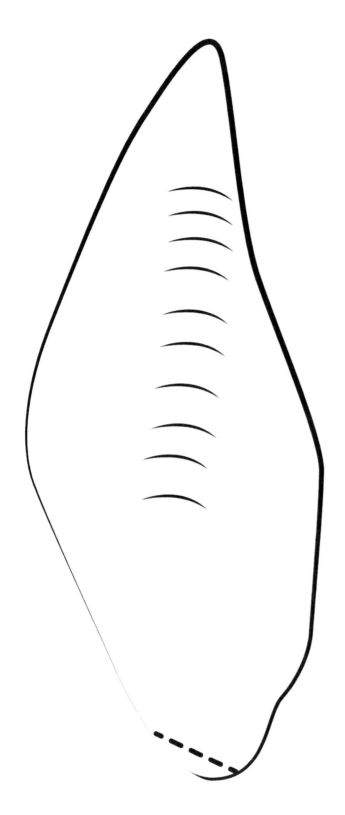

LEFT EAR

LEFT TRAGUS

© Be Naturally Curious, LLC. All rights reserved.

Greater spear-nosed bat

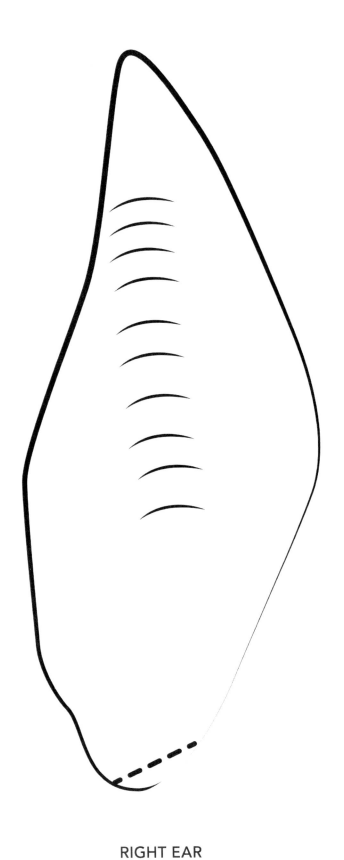

RIGHT EAR

RIGHT TRAGUS

© Be Naturally Curious, LLC. All rights reserved.

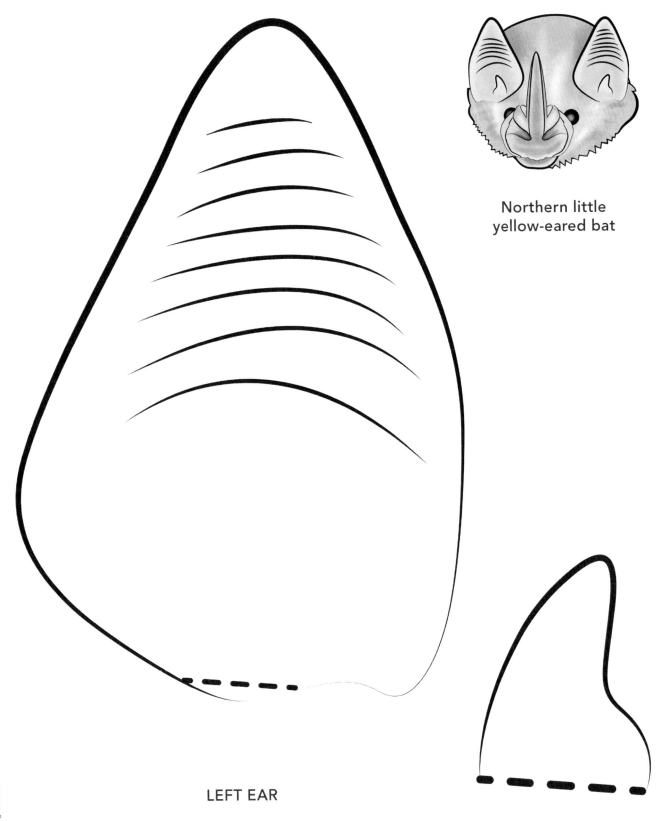

Northern little
yellow-eared bat

LEFT EAR

LEFT TRAGUS

© Be Naturally Curious, LLC. All rights reserved.

Northern little
yellow-eared bat

RIGHT EAR

RIGHT TRAGUS

© Be Naturally Curious, LLC. All rights reserved.

Bottlenose dolphin

DOLPHIN UPPER SNOUT
(identical to lower snout)

© Be Naturally Curious, LLC. All rights reserved.

Bottlenose dolphin

DOLPHIN LOWER SNOUT
(identical to upper snout)

© Be Naturally Curious, LLC. All rights reserved.

Orca

ORCA UPPER SNOUT

© Be Naturally Curious, LLC. All rights reserved.

Orca

ORCA LOWER SNOUT

© Be Naturally Curious, LLC. All rights reserved.

ECHOLOCATION ELEMENTS GAME

S C O R E C A R D

~ Save your cards here ~

The first player to collect all of the following _for the same animal_ wins:

2 body parts for creating sounds • 1 sound card
2 body parts for hearing echoes • 2 purposes for echolocating

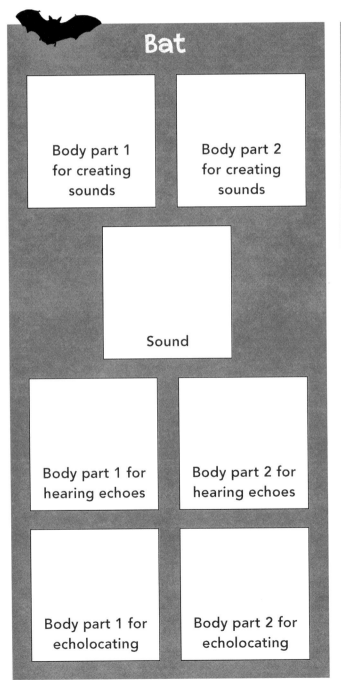

Bat

Body part 1 for creating sounds	Body part 2 for creating sounds
Sound	
Body part 1 for hearing echoes	Body part 2 for hearing echoes
Body part 1 for echolocating	Body part 2 for echolocating

Dolphin

Body part 1 for creating sounds	Body part 2 for creating sounds
Sound	
Body part 1 for hearing echoes	Body part 2 for hearing echoes
Body part 1 for echolocating	Body part 2 for echolocating

© Be Naturally Curious, LLC. All rights reserved.

ECHOLOCATION ELEMENTS GAME

SCORECARD

~ Save your cards here ~

The first player to collect all of the following _for the same animal_ wins:

2 body parts for creating sounds • 1 sound card
2 body parts for hearing echoes • 2 purposes for echolocating

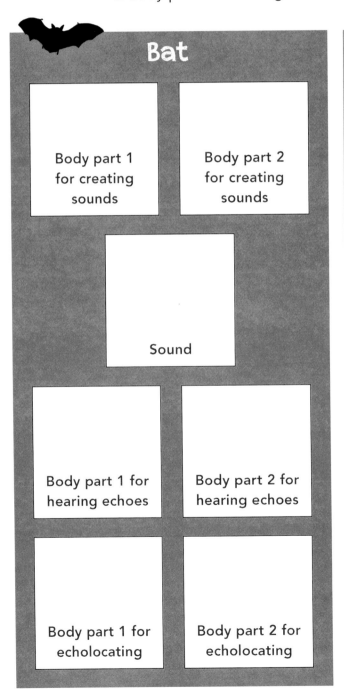

Bat

Body part 1 for creating sounds	Body part 2 for creating sounds
Sound	
Body part 1 for hearing echoes	Body part 2 for hearing echoes
Body part 1 for echolocating	Body part 2 for echolocating

Dolphin

Body part 1 for creating sounds	Body part 2 for creating sounds
Sound	
Body part 1 for hearing echoes	Body part 2 for hearing echoes
Body part 1 for echolocating	Body part 2 for echolocating

© Be Naturally Curious, LLC. All rights reserved.

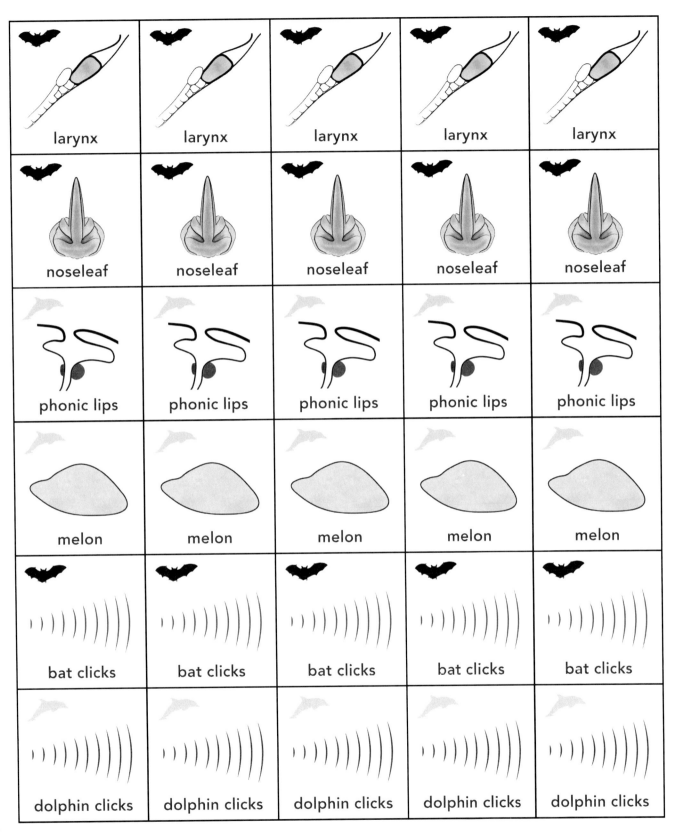

© Be Naturally Curious, LLC. All rights reserved.

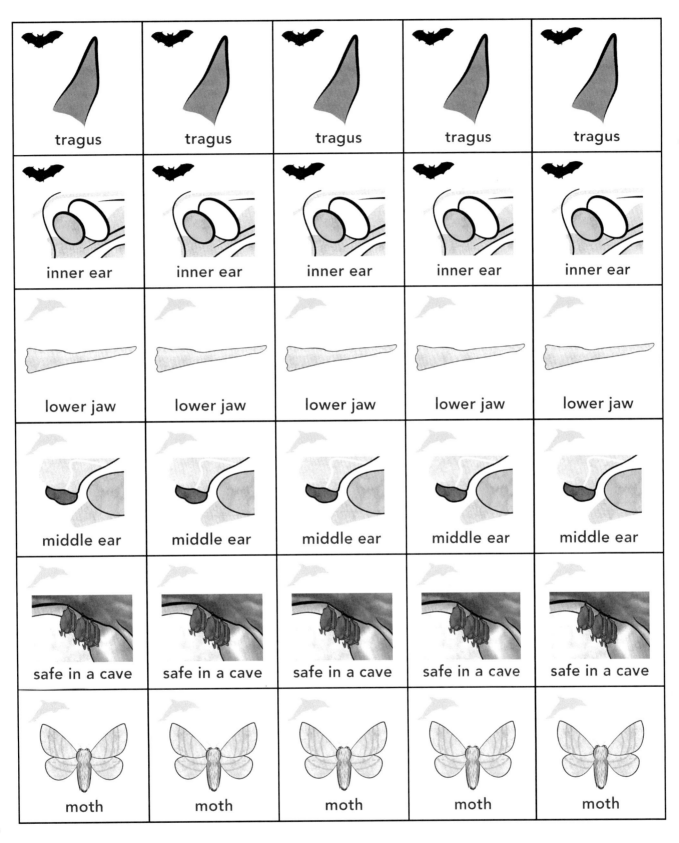

tragus   tragus   tragus   tragus   tragus

inner ear   inner ear   inner ear   inner ear   inner ear

lower jaw   lower jaw   lower jaw   lower jaw   lower jaw

middle ear   middle ear   middle ear   middle ear   middle ear

safe in a cave   safe in a cave   safe in a cave   safe in a cave   safe in a cave

moth   moth   moth   moth   moth

© Be Naturally Curious, LLC. All rights reserved.

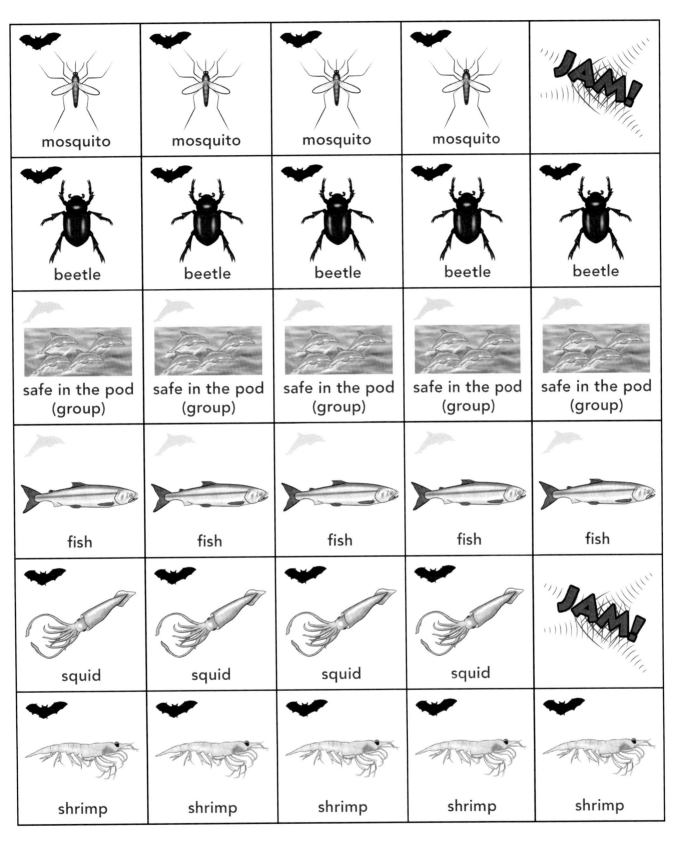

© Be Naturally Curious, LLC. All rights reserved.

ACTIVITY 3

Experimental Journal

Name of listener: _____

Sound #1	Listener	Actual
How was the sound made?		
Which direction did the sound come from?		
How far away was the sound?		
What else did you notice about the sound?		

Sound #2	Listener	Actual
How was the sound made?		
Which direction did the sound come from?		
How far away was the sound?		
What else did you notice about the sound?		

Sound #3	Listener	Actual
How was the sound made?		
Which direction did the sound come from?		
How far away was the sound?		
What else did you notice about the sound?		

© Be Naturally Curious, LLC. All rights reserved.

Cutouts for Activity 3: Name That Sound

ACTIVITY 3

Experimental Journal

Name of listener: _____

Sound #1	Listener	Actual
How was the sound made?		
Which direction did the sound come from?		
How far away was the sound?		
What else did you notice about the sound?		

Sound #2	Listener	Actual
How was the sound made?		
Which direction did the sound come from?		
How far away was the sound?		
What else did you notice about the sound?		

Sound #3	Listener	Actual
How was the sound made?		
Which direction did the sound come from?		
How far away was the sound?		
What else did you notice about the sound?		

© Be Naturally Curious, LLC. All rights reserved.

ACTIVITY 3

Experimental Journal

Name of listener: _____

Sound #1	Listener	Actual
How was the sound made?		
Which direction did the sound come from?		
How far away was the sound?		
What else did you notice about the sound?		

Sound #2	Listener	Actual
How was the sound made?		
Which direction did the sound come from?		
How far away was the sound?		
What else did you notice about the sound?		

Sound #3	Listener	Actual
How was the sound made?		
Which direction did the sound come from?		
How far away was the sound?		
What else did you notice about the sound?		

© Be Naturally Curious, LLC. All rights reserved.

© Be Naturally Curious, LLC. All rights reserved.

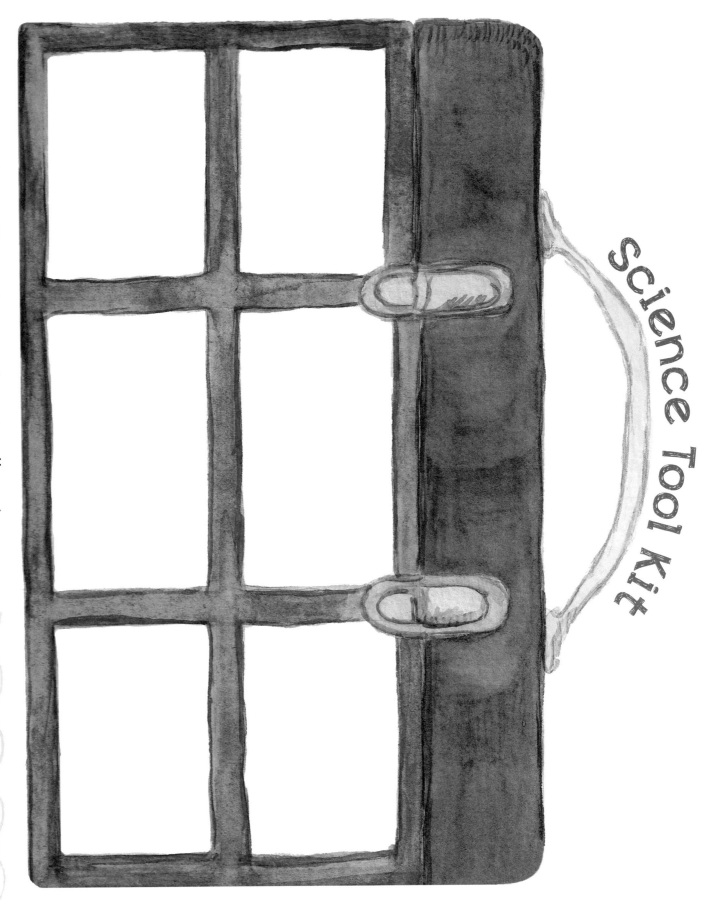

www.benaturallycurious.com

Science Tool Kit

43917450R00035

Made in the USA
Middletown, DE
22 May 2017